1991

WHAT MAKES A SCHOOL CATHOLIC?

Edited by:
Francis D. Kelly, S.T.L., Ph.D.

Published by
The National Catholic Educational Association

TABLE OF CONTENTS

INTRODUCTION

The Second Vatican Council itself gave an answer to the important question posed by this monograph: "What makes the Catholic school distinctive is its attempt to generate a community climate in the school that is permeated by the Gospel spirit of freedom and love...where personality development goes hand in hand with the development of the 'new creature' that each one has become through baptism. It tries to relate all of human culture to the goodness of salvation so that the light of faith will illumine everything that the students will gradually come to learn about the world, about life, and about the human person" (Declaration on Christian Education, #8).

In June of 1988, one hundred and eighty Catholic school educators met for a week at the University of Dayton at an Institute sponsored by the Departments of Religious Education and Secondary Schools of the National Catholic Educational Association to explore these issues. This monograph includes some of the papers presented at that meeting so that they may be of benefit to the tens of thousands of dedicated administrators and teachers who serve nearly 3 million young people in the Catholic school system in the United States.

The reader will find echoes in these pages of the conciliar goals mentioned above and an application of them to our particular situation about twenty five years later. Together with reflection on the goals the reader will also find suggestions for practical implementation in such areas as religion curriculum building, fostering students' prayer lives, encouraging commitment to Catholic social teaching.

The predominantly lay staffing that is now characteristic of our schools makes reflection on the question "What Makes a School Catholic?" ever more urgent. Many of the externals such as teachers in religious habits no longer provide an aura of Catholicism. It must be the kind of values reflected in the following pages that must suffuse the total school atmosphere and the entire staff that will alone guarantee the authentic Catholicity of the school. This means that administrators must give high priority to the selection and on-going spiritual support of staff who will share these ideas and communicate them effectively to their students.

May the Holy Spirit continue to inspire and direct Catholic educators in their privileged vocation of service!

Rev. Francis D. Kelly
Executive Director
Department of Religious Education

EVANGELIZING THE UNCONVERTED

William J. O'Malley, S.J.

A missionary in the Australian outback has it easier than a religious educator in a posh suburban school. I concede the missionary's physical discomforts—the ticks and leeches, the alligators, the dust, the curare-tipped blowdarts, the malaria. But at least he or she can say every night, "Some people didn't die today because of me." In contrast, the teacher here at home has most of the bland comforts of the middle class; there is little drama beyond an occasional stink bomb in the sophomore lockers, little nobility beyond the reassurance that "I did not kill Donald Dorgan today."

And yet there is a very dramatic and very noble struggle going on in our dust-free, air-conditioned paradises: the challenge to discomfit the comfy, to penetrate impenetrable smugness, to unnerve young people who are convinced that being spoiled is an incurable disease—but also convinced that they are good Christians because they are "nice." In brief, our task is to evangelize the baptized but unconverted. Don Quixote had it easier. At least windmills fought back.

I submit that it would be easier to convert a cannibal than to sell distributive justice to boys from Scarsdale and girls from Beverly Hills. You'd have a better chance selling acne.

What's more, if we are truly honest about our mandate, we are also trying to subvert precisely the two most precious hopes our students' parents have for them: first, that they have "the good life," and, second, that they not suffer.

We aren't visibly noble warriors, like the missionary in the outback, but there is an unsung nobility and drama to our lives. John LeCarre and Martin Cruz and Len Deighton could write novels about us. We are the Church's moles, her double-agents, her subversives.

OUR PURPOSE

If you asked our parents why they don't take advantage of their school-tax money, I imagine many would answer, "Catholic schools have better discipline." If that's what they're after, their children would have gotten even better discipline in the Marines. Not to mention prison. If that's all they want for children in Catholic schools—to be self-disciplined, upwardly mobile, to assure them of

Rev. William O'Malley, S.J. teaches religion at Fordham Preparatory School, the Bronx, New York, and is a frequent contributor to *America* on the issue of adolescent religious education.

"the good things in life" (*viz:* a six-figure job, a swimming pool, and a video-cassette recorder), then all our lay faculties should be chalking up more money and fewer headaches working in munitions factories, and all the religious should say with Jerry Starrat, "Get yourselves another set of vestal virgins."

Catholic schools aren't there to make our young upwardly mobile. Nor to assure them of a wrinkle-free life. Nor to offer them security. They're there precisely to take all that *away* from them. They're there to lure them to give *up* security and come out onto the road. Any school that claims to embody the gospel of Jesus Christ must, by definition, try (most of the time in vain) to subvert all the siren songs our young ever heard from the Electronic Babysitter, and make them the apostles they were ordained to be at baptism, an apostleship they themselves allegedly confirmed at Confirmation.

Despite all those years of what they still call "Catholic brainwashing," our children believe being a Christian means (a) not hurting anybody and (b) being nice to people. But how would that make a Christian any different from a good Jew or an ethical atheist? They don't want to hurt people either; they want to be nice, too. But they're not Christians.

Again, our children think Christianity has something to do only with morality: no abortion, no pimping, no pushing drugs. No, no, no. Christianity is not primarily about morality—except insofar as Christianity *presumes* morality. Jews have to be moral; Moslems have to be moral. Christianity has no monopoly on morality. One has to be moral merely to be *human*. Once you're there, at the level of humanity, then you may have a chance to hear the call to be Christian.

OUR PRODUCT

Humanity is our nature; it's natural. Christianity is humanity-plus; it's supernatural. Christianity doesn't ask us to be unbad; it asks us to be holy. But I'd wager that 99.7% of your students would as soon be called a bad name as be called "holy." And yet, when Jesus or any Jew said "holy," they didn't mean "pious." They meant "whole," or—in the modern patois, "having all your act together." You know who you are and where you're going.

We want to lead our students with ourselves to acknowledge—humbly—that we are not God, and yet we also acknowledge—proudly—that we have been chosen. That we are his sons and daughters, peers of the realm. That we have been *missioned*, just as Jesus was missioned. At this moment, Jesus has no hands but our hands. He has no hearts but our hearts. We are his embodiment. This is the life-ideal a Catholic school wants to present to its students.

The call of the Christian is to serve, to be used, especially by the undeserving. If we are peers of the realm, then *noblesse oblige*. We have it on the highest authority that the *only* norm for "the good life" is not, on the one hand, how high your SAT's were, or how much money you made, or how many times you got your name in the papers. We have it from Jesus himself that the only question which will determine whether your life was worth living is: "I was hungry. I was thirsty. I was the one they called 'nerd.' What did you *do* about that?"

If our young find that gospel message boring and not unnerving, then our young have never really heard the gospel message.

So: that's the intimidating product we offer. And it is the touchstone by which our schools will be judged Catholic or not.

And what is the audience to whom we offer it? Not just: "the young," but *these* young—who have a very disquieting point when they say, "You were *never* my age."

OUR AUDIENCE

Our audience is convinced that, within ten years of college graduation, they will be living at least as well as their parents; that the Yellow Brick Road stretches inexorably before them toward Oz; that being spoiled is an incurable disease. As in *1984*, they are already adept at using Soma, recreational sex, thought control, and double-think. It's nearly impossible to lure self-absorbed egotists to an act of faith. God? One is doing quite splendidly without him, thank you. Where's the profit?

BUT, paradoxically, the young people to whom we are missioned are also—at one and the same time—precisely the *opposite* of world-beating egotists. They are deadly (and I use the word advisedly) aware of their own shortcomings. It's almost as if Arnold Schwartznegger had taken the spectrum and twisted it into a hoop, so that our young could be *both* egotistical *and* paranoid at the same time—which is precisely the classical definition of narcissism: Oz is, at one and the same time, inevitable and impossible.

For the paranoid, everything on earth is a mirror, testifying unarguably and ceaselessly to his or her shortcomings: the commercials, the Little League tryouts, the SAT's, the mugger, the Joneses. What in my youth was a dispiriting deluge of guilt has turned into a gluey morass of formless anxieties. Paranoids are humbled to the point of paralysis. And yet, with pathetic irony, the abjectly humble also try to grab center stage and monologize their faults, deifying their ineptitude, refusing to surrender the job of being perfect to Someone Else. It's nearly impossible to lead a paranoid to an act of faith. God? Where's the guarantee?

As C.S. Lewis said, the Enemy of Human Nature need not corrupt our youngsters into axe murderers or potentates of porn or genocides. All he has to do is give them a mirror. And they have plenty of mirrors; many we ourselves have handed to them. Whether they are mesmerized with reflections of their own indomitable charms or

5

with reflections of their own ineradicable shortcomings, the result is the same: they are paralyzed.

Tell that audience of narcissists: "If you want the first place, take the last place." Tell that audience: "if you have two coats, and your brother has none, give your brother one of your coats." Tell that audience: "If you want to be truly fulfilled, forget security and come out on the road with Me." To the Me Generation, in the world of monopoly capitalism, that's equivalent to suggesting deicide.

THE CAUSES

What brought all this about? Why is the gospel so unappealing? Why—to give only one concrete example—are vacations more important than vocations? Why have vocations in America dropped by two-thirds in fifteen years? And yet, in places like Eastern Europe and the Third World, vocations are looking healthier and healthier. Keep that in mind. There may be a clue there.

When searching out the culprit who stole the fire from our churches and schools, we can look to Claude Rain's classic command in "Casablanca": "Round up the usual suspects." And there they all stand: television, *Playboy*, Madison Avenue, the Pill, the stockholders of the Trojan Condom Corporation, the marijuana and cocaine peddlers, and all those garish Heavy Metal rockers who look like storm troopers in drag.

But in that unseemly line-up, let us not be too humble to allow prominent places to ourselves, as a Church and as individual parents and teachers.

If we can lower our defenses and see the objective truth, our Church puts on a rather lackluster show compared to our more professional opposition, a liturgy whose script even Danny Kaye couldn't bring to life; the hymns are pastel paeans to a God who always cherishes and hardly ever challenges, twanged out on guitars which make the Trinity as folksy as the Bartles brothers; the homily—not always, but far too often—is a twenty-minute ramble consisting mostly of detours. The majority of high school students I've taught, most of them from parochial schools, seem to have been given a gospel emptied of any challenge, a concept of Christianity I have belabored elsewhere as "Jesus, the Warm Fuzzy." If they read the secular or diocesan press, they see what appears at least to me (and I'm 100% committed) the embarrassing scandal of people on our own side of the barricades lobbing grenades at one another.

But all the fault is not with the institutional Church. I think it is also rooted—again paradoxically—in the good intentions of American Catholic parents. I think Catholic parents have, unwittingly, defused the Gospel by trying to shield their children from a reality which is not only the bedrock of the gospel but also the *sine qua non* of achieving even an integral humanity: the experience of suffering.

SUFFERING

If there are two qualities any of us would think of immediately as norms for a good parent, they would be, first, to provide the best one could for one's children—the best food, clothes, home, education—and, second, to do one's damnedest to see that they don't get hurt. Laudable, but I wonder, aloud, if providing the best and shielding from suffering may not be questionable gifts.

More than a few fathers have said to me, "I made up my mind that my kids weren't going to have to wade through all the crap I had to wade through as a kid—two jobs, jealousy of the other kids' clothes and cars and summer vacation places. So, I did it, by God. I gave them everything I never had...except the one thing I did get from wading through all that crap: spine."

We live in an age which abhors the idea even of inconvenience, much less the idea of suffering. Just think of what would happen, for instance, if all the electricity in your house went out for a week. And yet, we have it—again on the highest testimony—that no one can avoid suffering. The Son of God himself, demonstrably, didn't. But we forget, even though we've had one in our homes since we were children, that *the* symbol which embodies the whole meaning of Christianity is a statue of a corpse. St. Paul emphatically reminded the first Christians: "Jews demand 'signs' and Greeks look for 'wisdom' but we preach Christ crucified!" (1 Cor. 1:22-23)

What's more, the entire history of humankind has shown that men and women can achieve their full humanity—freedom, and dignity—*only* by coming to terms with suffering. Life is difficult. Every philosopher from Buddha to Karl Marx started from that fundamental and indisputable fact. Until you start there, you haven't started. But there is the fact most middle-class adolescents are shielded from: that suffering is a natural factor in human life—and in human growth. What's more, it is unavoidable; it will arise from the imperfect way in which we are made and from interactions with other different, self-willed, imperfect persons. One has to consider only one of many indisputable truths: you can't make anyone love you more than he or she is able.

The question is not whether life is difficult or not. That is a given. The question is whether you're going to try to solve it or just sit there and moan about it.

Carl Jung said, "Neurosis is always a substitute for legitimate suffering." In order to avoid facing the truth about life and about ourselves, we escape to games: senioritis, shyness, perfectionism, etc., flying directly in the face of the facts. Like playing volleyball in a minefield. In the first place, because of the natures of things and human beings, the substitutes are most often more painful than the painful truth. In the second place, in avoiding suffering, we avoid growth. If you ask the question why children whom most people in the world would consider spoiled commit suicide, you already have the answer right in your question. They've been given to believe that life and human beings will deliver what no life and no human being can deliver.

And if, over and above humanity, we want our young to achieve Christianity—to spend their lives as men and women for others—suffering has to be transformed into willing and open-handed sacrifice, which ennobles both the receiver and the giver.

We want our children to be happy. But today, being happy is totally subjective, a feeling; if you *feel* happy, you are happy. The Greeks were wiser, I think. The Greek word for happiness—*eudaimonia*—means a good spirit, a good soul. To be happy is not to feel good but to be good. According to that definition, as Scott Peck says, prisoners trudging to the gas ovens with their chins high were happy. Hitler kicking up his heels at the humiliation of France was not happy.

Now, I'm not recommending that Catholic parents seclude themselves in the cellar and dream up Dickensian torments for their children: hair shirts, spiders in their beds, BBs in their Cheerios. Nor am I suggesting that they throw out all their clothes and stereos and videogames. But I am suggesting that, if our children are not involved in some kind of selfless service for others—no matter what their age—then there is a major need for painful rethinking.

CATHOLIC SCHOOLS

What, then, makes a school Catholic? Not the crucifix on the roof, surely, nor the presence of a chapel, no matter how imposing. Let me answer the question, in true Hibernian fashion, with more questions:

— Are there as many students in your service programs as there are on your varsity teams? In order to get the whole student body involved in the service programs, would you have to make them requirements for graduation? Are those programs something the parents demand of their children and of the school?

— Is there a serious collateral program of reflection with the service program—a journal, say—which forces students to see their service to the suffering Body of Christ?

— If there is such a reflection program, how many of the faculty are involved in it? If not all, is there a substantive reason? What other priorities are offered—and accepted—as excuses not to participate?

— Is your retreat budget as large as your athletic budget? If not, then your whole theology program, no matter how professional, is quite likely as academic as history or math.

— Are your retreats (at least after the initial ones to cut the ice) genuine attempts to lead students to center themselves and open themselves to communications with God? To allow the scriptures to subvert the expectations of human fulfillment bred into them by uncountable hours of materialist brainwashing? Or

8

are they merely huggy-kissy-touchy-feely group-gropes?

— Are all the faculty and staff, without exception, genuine Christian apostles? Is that part of their job interview, at least as important as their academic credentials? Can they be expected to help out routinely with liturgies, retreats, service projects? Or do they gripe about having periods shortened to allow for Mass or confessions?

If your operation isn't perfect, there's hardly need to worry. A few moment's reflection on the success of the first Christian school—the twelve apostles—should dispel any hopes of immediate success. The real question is which direction you are headed in. And how many of the leaders are marching in precisely the opposite direction: toward the M.B.A. and the Superbowl Trophy and the star in the sidewalk outside Grauman's Chinese Theater?

Those of us in Catholic education have two very formidable challenges, neither of which will go away: our children and the gospel. Even though it seems that all the king's horses and all the king's men can't make these twain meet—I don't know about you, but I can't wait to get back each September to try again!

A CATHOLIC TRADITION OF CONTEMPLATION

Fr. Thomas Keating, O.C.S.O.

One might wonder why a Trappist monk would be involved in a workshop on Catholic secondary education! Actually I myself am a student. St Benedict, in his Rule for monks, calls the monastery a "school of the Lord's service"—a school from which you never quite graduate. In addition, it is my experience that every person of whatever age has a transcendent dimension that is waiting to be activated.

I wonder if to awaken the transcendent or contemplative dimension of the young is not, in fact, the principal challenge and contribution of a Catholic school?

Catholic identity is forged by persons who are "alive to God in Christ Jesus" (Rm 6: 11) and not so much by dogmas or observances. Catholicism is a living tradition of faith and life. The Judaism of Jesus' time had distorted the living tradition of the covenant and Jesus' mission was to restore the transcendent dimension as the prophets had done before him. A similar challenge faces the Church in every period of history. This is what authentic renewal is all about.

In the course of participating in East-West dialogue, I have visited Hindu and Buddhist communities. At least half the people one meets in these communities are former Catholics who were turned off on the parish level or in Catholic schools because they never heard about contemplative spirituality. They didn't even know it existed in the Christian tradition because it was never talked about.

A priest told me that in the seminary when the text book came to the subject of contemplation, the professor said, "We can skip all this; this is for the boys at the Trappist monastery behind the walls. You can forget it."

The idea that contemplative prayer belongs only to professional contemplatives living a special lifestyle is an illusion. The contemplative dimension of the Gospel is its most essential element. The Gospel is the story of Christ's experience of Ultimate Reality as Abba, the God of infinite caring and compassion. The same experience is being communicated in the sacraments, prayer and every Christian devotion. It is out of the contemplative dimension that empowerment for social action emerges.

Rev. Thomas A. Keating, O.C.S.O. is a monk of St. Benedict's Trappist Cistercian Abbey, Snowmass, CO, and a founder of the Contemplative Prayer movement in the United States.

There are a significant number of ordinary Christians who feel the need for a deeper life of prayer and some kind of structure to support it. This is the particular ministry that Contemplative Outreach addresses. Almost every parish that offers a contemplative prayer workshop finds that a certain number of people have been waiting, perhaps for years, to hear about this kind of spiritual development.

As a Catholic educator, how consciously do you orient your students toward the person of Christ? The Gospel as a living tradition is primarily a relationship with Christ. We may think of prayer as words or thoughts that describe inner feelings. But it is a much broader umbrella than that. When the celebrant says, "Let us pray," what is he saying? "Let's have a relationship with God;" or "let's improve the one we have;" or "let's celebrate the one we are experiencing."

Theology teaches that in baptism we receive everything we need to be transformed. Remember the package: the four infused virtues, the three theological virtues, the seven gifts of the Spirit and the indwelling of the Trinity. We have these tremendous gifts from the moment of baptism. Yet we place so little confidence in this incredible energy. Shouldn't Catholic education be designed to release that energy and teach students how to use it so that they may gradually assimilate and be assimilated to the Word of God?

There is general awareness that average human consciousness may be moving to a new level. This creates an opening to challenge students to a heightened spiritual awareness and action.

The contemplative tradition has been lost in the Church at large since the Reformation. In order to avoid doctrinal errors, the counter-Reformation placed great emphasis on doctrinal formulations and their correct transmission. Anything suggesting personal inspiration was thought to be suspect. These trends had a devastating impact on the Church's contemplative tradition.

Without the goal of personal transformation, Christian life is truncated. It is something else. When students are oriented to the person of Christ, they can then see the institutional Church in the service of that transformation. This is to see it from the inside.

In the Eastern tradition the guru is believed to have the enlightenment that the disciple would like to possess. The capacity for enlightenment is believed to be present in the disciple. The guru's job is to awaken the enlightenment that is latent in the individual. In the course of the training there is a gradual transmission of the understanding of the teacher to the disciple.

LITURGY AND LECTIO DIVINA

How does this transmission take place in Christianity where teachers are themselves only disciples? Christ is the guru, the one master: the enlightened One. How do we receive the mind of Christ? The liturgy, rightly understood and celebrated, is the principle place of transmission. When we are prepared for the communication of divine life, light and love, the liturgy becomes the hallowed place of transmission.

It is not, however, the only place where the mystery of Christ is communicated. "Lectio divina" is another place that tradition has hallowed. It disposes one for liturgy and its practice as a prolongation of the encounter with Christ in the sacraments. A major way of awakening the transcendent potential of students might be to introduce them to the practice of "lectio divina." The reading of the gospels as "lectio divina" is not for the sake of learning something but of getting acquainted with Jesus Christ. The texts provide the topics of conversation. "Lectio divina" means "reading in an attitude of listening to the word of God," as a direct encounter with Jesus. You read until a word or thought strikes you, and then you put the text down and allow your reflections to unfold.

In the course of reflecting you may want to respond to the good things that you are reading about with particular acts such as admiration, gratitude, hope, praise or petition. Your emotions begin to reinforce your acts of will. As long as the outpourings of your heart continue, there is no need to return to the text or to continue reflecting.

On the other hand, when your reflections or particular acts have run their course, return to the text. You may read only a few more sentences when the same process begins again. In this way, you slowly weave your way through the text, assimilating the teaching and example of Jesus with the heart as well as with the mind.

After you have practiced "lectio divina" regularly, your responses to the example and teaching of Jesus you are reading and reflecting about may simplify to a single sentence or phrase that sums up your understanding, gratitude and affection for Jesus. Your conversation is now opening to the level of communion.

The holy Spirit who inspired the sacred writers is also within us. Under the Spirit's influence, we begin to taste something of the goodness of God. In the Middle Ages this experience was called "resting in God." It is the experience of God's presence arising from deep within or enveloping us from without.

Suppose we keep up this practice of spending time and hanging out with Christ. It turns into a friendlier relationship. You begin to feel more at ease. On the other hand, if we don't persevere in cultivating the acquaintanceship, it doesn't go anywhere. Fortunately, God is not vindictive. If we don't turn up for the interview, he says, "Okay, if you're not ready, I'll wait for you; I'm not going anywhere." God waits for us, but we lose the time during which we could have made immense progress in the relationship.

PRAYER AND TRANSFORMATION

Prayer develops like other relationships. Give it time and priority and it grows of itself. The early Fathers of the Church recognized that after the period of acquaintanceship and friendliness, there would be a crisis just as there is in any relationship. The crisis consists in asking, "Where is this going? Will I be disappointed or betrayed? Fear enters in and we back off. God will not let us get into this friendship without our realizing what is involved and making a choice. The love of friendship is not a one way street. It involves a willingness to give as well as to get. Friendship always involves commitment. You can walk away from a casual relationship. You cannot walk away from friendship without breaking hearts. This kind of commitment to Christ has been institutionalized in religious vows and the reception of the sacrament of orders. However, our baptismal vocation to Jesus and to transformation in Christ takes precedence over every particular way of living that commitment.

A paradigm for the practice of "lectio divina" is Mary of Bethany sitting at the feet of Jesus listening to his words (Lk 10:38-42). She is also listening at a deeper level to the person (Jesus) who is speaking and resting in the love of Christ. This is the movement of "lectio divina" and it leads more and more to "centering prayer"—the practice of silently resting in God's love. To teach religion without giving students a personal prayer practice is to give students just another course. The dogmas of the Church are pointers to the Ultimate Mystery. They are not the mystery itself.

Many people are arrested at the reasoning and analyzing process and resist the attraction of grace to move beyond thinking to resting in the presence of Christ. To this "rest" Jesus invites us saying, "Come to me, all you who are weary and find life burdensome, and I will refresh you" (Mt 11:28). It is from the personal love of Christ that service spontaneously emerges. The energy is too great to sit on. One sees Christ in "the least of the brothers and sisters" and must bear witness to his resurrection by manifesting his love in daily life.

As teachers in Catholic schools we have the opportunity and the challenge to open our students to the spiritual and transcendent dimension of their faith. If we succeed we have made a life-long contribution to their development. In the midst of the stresses of life they will never forget Augustine's dictum: "You have made us for Yourself O God, and our hearts will find no rest until they rest in you."

CATHOLIC IDENTITY AND THE CHURCH:
IS THE CHURCH A PROBLEM FOR OUR STUDENTS?
Rev. James Heft, S.M.

The challenge the religion teacher in a Catholic school faces today is that of bringing students to understand the Church as their spiritual home, as a place where they and God meet, and as a "pillar and bulwark of truth" (1 Tm. 3:15) as the New Testament pastoral puts it.

Every teacher knows that there are many cultural, social and even theological obstacles to helping our young people come to a positive attitude towards the Church.

Before addressing this challenge I would make two preliminary points:

1. We do not want to focus our Catholic identity in a triumphalistic manner or to foster invidious comparisons with other Christian groups. We do not want to turn our students into intolerant ideologues or smug separatists. Rather, the ecumenical spirit fostered by the Second Vatican Council should shape our attitudes about the Church and about the value of other churches and religions.

2. In speaking about Catholic identity we need to realize that Catholic identity is broad enough to be pictured as an "umbrella" under which a significant amount of healthy pluralism may be found. There are, however, definite boundaries to the right and to the left, ahead and behind, but within those boundaries there is much room for diversity.

To illustrate this point let me share with you a technique I use with my college students. I teach a course entitled "Catholic Doctrines" for which I have two large textbooks—one written by a theologian I would describe as a reasonable liberal, Richard McBrien (*Catholicism*) and the other by a responsible conservative, John Hardon (*The Catechism*). Both theologians, I believe, would describe themselves as in the mainstream of Catholic thought; however, I think my description of them as liberal and conservative, both still orthodox, is basically fair. When we study each doctrine, we read both books and discuss the different ways in which each author develops his points. I have found this to be for the students an enriching study of legitimate Catholic pluralism.

Rev. James L. Heft, S.M. is Provost of the University of Dayton, Dayton, OH.

THE DEVELOPMENT OF ECCLESIOLOGY

The study of the Church, as an explicit theological subject in itself, is really a relatively recent development in the history of the Church. Ecclesiology, as a separate focus of study, did not exist before the fourteenth century. At this time, controversies between the Church and the state, and conflicts over the respective roles and powers of the pope and the princes provided theologians and particularly canon lawyers, with a need to clarify the nature and limits of the authority of the Church and the state.

In the sixteenth century, the Protestant Reformation forced the Church to develop a more explicit ecclesiology. The Reformers had emphasized the invisible nature of the Church as a community of the pre-destined. The Catholic Church, in response, emphasized its visible, institutional nature. St. Robert Bellarmine produced what became for centuries the classic definition of the Church as a visible society, as visible as the Republic of Venice, instituted by Christ and under the direction of the Pope.

In the hands of less able theologians than Bellarmine, the distinction between a visible and invisible distinction became polarized. People forgot what Augustine once said: that all those whom the Church has, God does not have; and all those whom God has, the Church does not have. Instead, many Catholic apologists tended to identify the Church and the kingdom of God, making it more and more difficult to see the Church as sinful and always in need of reform. In the nineteenth century, particularly through the work of Johann Adam Mohler (1796-1838) in Germany and John Henry Newman (1801-1890) in England, the Church began to reacquire a more living sense of tradition and the possibility of change.

Pope Pius XII, through his great encyclical letter on the Church, *Mystici Corporis*, moved thinking about the Church away from a primarily juridical approach towards a more spiritual and organic approach. Through this important encyclical and others, Pius XII opened the door for the Second Vatican Council and its landmark Dogmatic Constitution on the Church, *Lumen Gentium*.

Vatican II's constitution on the Church devotes its first chapter to the mystery of the Church—how God and humanity come together. In describing the Church as a mystery, the Council did not intend to dispense us from intellectual rigor but instead asked us to think more rigorously about the reality of the Church which escapes easy formulations.

THE ESSENCE OF CATHOLICISM

I believe that one of the best contemporary descriptions of the essence of Catholicism has been given by Richard McBrien. He highlights three inter-related realities: sacramentality, mediation and community. I believe his description is worth quoting at length, for few theologians today rival McBrien for comprehensive and lucid summaries of the central traditions of Catholicism:

> No theological principle or focus is more characteristic of Catholicism or more central to its identity than the principle of *sacramentality*. The Catholic vision sees God in and through all things: other people, communities, movements, events, places, objects, the world at large, the whole cosmos. The visible, the tangible, the finite, the historical—all these are actual or potential carriers of the divine presence. Indeed, it is only in and through these material realities that we can even encounter the invisible God. The great sacrament of our encounter with God and of God's encounter with us is Jesus Christ. The Church, in turn, is the sacrament of our encounter with Christ and of Christ's with us, and the sacraments, in turn, are the signs and instruments by which that ecclesial encounter with Christ is expressed, celebrated, and made effective for the glory of God and the salvation of men and women.
>
> A corollary of the principle of sacramentality is the principle of *mediation*. A sacrament not only signifies; it also causes what it signifies. Thus, created realities not only contain, reflect, or embody the presence of God, they make that presence effective for those who avail themselves of these realities. The universe of grace is a mediated reality: mediated principally by Christ, secondarily by the Church and by other signs and instruments of salvation outside and beyond the Church.
>
> Catholicism rejects naive realism, which holds to the immediacy of the experience of God as the normal or exclusive kind of encounter with the divine presence. Catholicism also rejects idealism, which holds that the encounter with God occurs solely in the inwardness of conscience and the inner recesses of consciousness. Catholicism holds, on the contrary, that the encounter with God is a mediated experience but a real experience, rooted in the historical and affirmed as real by the critical and systematic judgment that God is truly present and active here or there, in this event or that, in this person or that, in this object or that.
>
> Finally, Catholicism affirms the principle of *communion*: that our way to God and God's way to us is not only a mediated way but a communal way. And even when the divine-human encounter is most personal and individual, it is still communal in that the encounter is made possible by the mediation of the community. Thus, there is *not* simply an individual personal relationship with God or Jesus Christ that is established and sustained by mediative reflection on Sacred Scripture, for the Bible itself is the Church's book and is the testimony of the Church's original faith. The mystic (even in the narrow sense of the word) relies on language, ideas, concepts, presuppositions when he or she enters into, or reflects upon an intimate, contemplative relationship with God. We are radical social beings; our use of language is clear evidence of that. There is no relationship with God, however intense, profound, and unique, that dispenses entirely with the communal context of every human relationship with God (*Catholicism*, Winston Press, 1981, pp. 1180-81).

If, as McBrien states, Catholicism is at its core sacramental, mediated and communal, then it is obvious why the mystery of the Church ought to play such a central role in the Catholic's understanding and experience of God and Christian discipleship. The Church itself becomes a sort of sacrament, a visible community of faith in which the mysteries of salvation are mediated through the

16

liturgy of the sacraments. Moreover, the Church includes in its membership not just those now alive on earth, but all those gone before us marked with the sign of faith. It is they to whom the Church looks as an indication of the perfect communion with and in God to which the whole of humankind is called. The Catholic's sense of sacramentality begins with a sense of creation, with material reality as a sign of God's incredible creativity and awesome beauty. Instead of dwelling only on humanity's sinfulness, Catholicism also directs our attention to humanity's participation in God's life, in his freedom, intelligence and creativity.

According to McBrien, Protestantism by contrast has had, as a religious tradition that has emphasized the word, a certain uneasiness about the arts. Citing the modern Church historian of the University of Chicago, Lutheran Martin Marty, McBrien explains that Protestantism hesitates to sculpt and paint images of the interaction of God and humanity for fear that humanity's attention would be drawn away from God who remains invisible and beyond our senses. Marty has written that Protestantism "has often and maybe even usually been uneasy about unrestricted bodily attention, and has rather consistently feared the ecstacy of the dance through most of the years of its history" (Martin Marty, *Protestantism*, p. 228; for a broader view of Catholicism's aesthetical impact, see Kenneth Clark's *Civilization*, pp. 167-192, cited by McBrien, p. 1182).

Another Protestant theologian, this time, Baptist theologian Langdon Gilkey, also from the University of Chicago, offers us a sympathetic and insightful portrait of Catholicism. He mentions four. First on his list is Catholicism's "sense of reality, importance and 'weight' of tradition and history in the formation of his people and so of her religious truths, religious experience, and human wisdom." Newman once remarked that to be deeply immersed in history is to cease to be a Protestant. Put another way, the longer one's memory is, the more likely one is to value continuity and to draw from history a variety of rich and diverse insights.

Second, Gilkey, following McBrien's emphasis on the importance of the community and Catholicism's positive appreciation of created reality, remarks that in Catholicism, especially for a Protestant like himself, there is "a remarkable sense of humanity and grace in the communal life of Catholics... Consequently the love of life, the appreciation of the body and the senses, of joy and celebration, the tolerance of the sinner, these natural, worldly and 'human' virtues are far more clearly and universally embodied in Catholics and in Catholic life than in Protestants and in Protestantism."

Thirdly, Gilkey sees in the history of the Catholic tradition, a uniquely rich embodiment, when compared to other forms of western Christianity, of an experience of the pervasive "presence of God and of grace mediated through symbols to the entire course of ordinary human life." For Gilkey, a symbol points to and communicates the reality of God which lies beyond it. A symbol can unite "sensual, aesthetic and intellectual experience more readily than the experiences of proclamation or of an ecstatic spiritual presence." In Gilkey's view, the sacramental sensibility of the Catholic tradition "may provide the best entrance into a new synthesis of the Christian tradition with the vitalities as well as the relativities of contemporary existence."

Fourth and finally, Gilkey discerns within Catholicism throughout history "a drive toward rationality, the insistence that the divine mystery manifest in tradition and sacramental presence be insofar as possible penetrated, defended, and explicitated by the most acute rational reflection" (*Catholicism Confronts Modernity: A Protestant View*, pp. 17-18, 20-22, cited by McBrien, pp. 1182-1183).

THE MARKS OF THE CHURCH

If one were to expand these descriptions of Catholicism to include the work of other theologians, such as Avery Dulles (see his recent *The Catholicity of the Church*, Oxford Press, 1985, especially his introduction, first and last chapters) or Francis Sullivan (*The Church We Believe In*, Paulist Press, 1988, especially his first) a still richer appreciation of how to articulate what is unique and characteristic about the identity of the Catholic Church. I recommend that the reader study these books, and others, such as the very readable works of professor Lawrence Cunningham and the recent gracefully written Oxford paperback, *The Catholic Faith* (1986) written by Roderick Strange. Ten years ago there was a dearth of sound and accessible books about Catholic identity; now, we are blessed by having a number of such excellent books.

Before taking up the question of how best to handle some of the problems that arise when teaching about the Church today, I want to return briefly to a more traditional way of thinking about the Church. In the Nicene Creed, we describe the Church as "one, holy, catholic, apostolic." Our students should know these "marks" of the Church, and have some understanding of how for more traditional ecclesiology they delineate the essential characteristics of the Church. A brief comment on each of the four marks will underscore the ways in which thinking about the Church in this way also helps us grasp the true identity of the Church.

ONE

The Catholic Church stresses a visible unity that transcends all divisions of class, language, culture and nationality. There was in the Catholic Church in recent centuries a tendency to stress the need only for uniformity. In the Post-Vatican II Church there has been an effort to allow for greater inculturation—to give more latitude for the regional churches to express the Gospel in their own cultural forms. This must be done while preserving overall unity. The process inevitably will involve some tension. We see this reflected in the discussions between the Vatican and some African churches about liturgical experimentation and again, with South American theologians, over some form of theology of liberation.

This tension is built into the very nature of the Church as a mystery of unity that of necessity admits of a certain pluriformity. We need to help students understand this. Actually, we need to come to grips with this better ourselves. A grasp of the Church's unity (not uniformity) can help eliminate negative caricatures which portray Church authorities as always resisting change and thwarting local autonomy. We should help our students see this tension as a graced on-going dialogue built into the very nature of the Church as truly Catholic.

HOLY

Some forms of Protestantism hold that although faith prevents our sinful guilt from being imputed to us, we nonetheless remain sinful in ourselves. This view is especially found among evangelicals and fundamentalists. In such a view of salvation positive view of the sanctification that has come to us through Christ's passion and death. We realize, and need to stress (for it is sometimes overlooked in preaching and teaching) that salvation is a gift. But as Catholics we have a very rich appreciation of the way in which it truly renews us inwardly and even "divinizes" us. The Eastern Catholic and Orthodox churches have been especially rich in their grasp and expression of this truth.

APOSTOLIC

While Protestants have tended to define apostolicity as adherence to the Gospel message set forth in Scripture, Catholics have tended to emphasize "apostolic succession" in episcopal office by historical continuity in the laying on of hands. The current ecumenical dialogue between the various Christian churches is helping both churches to see the importance of the other's perspective—we need to see apostolicity in terms both of fidelity to the gospel message and integrity of office.

CATHOLICITY

Never more than today, when the world is experienced as a "global village," is this mark of the Church important. The Roman Catholic Church, as the only true transnational, trans-cultural world institution is in a wonderful position to be a prophetic force for witnessing to the saving truth, and standing firmly for human rights, justice and peace. We need to broaden our students' horizons to appreciate this dimension of the Church.

INSTITUTIONAL CHURCH: A PROBLEM

The danger of the very phrase "institutional Church" is that it almost always is the catch-all phrase used to refer to anything that strikes them negatively. Martin Marty has recently published an insightful article ("You're Going to Have to be Institutionalized," in *The Critic*, 43 (1989), #4) in which he notes that from young people one typically hears that they believe in God and love Jesus, but that they just find the Church boring. He plays on the *American Heritage Dictionary* second and third definitions of the word "institutionalize." The second meaning is "to continue (a person) to an institution." When used in this sense to describe the Church, we picture the Church as an asylum or a prison. The third meaning is "to expose to the harmful effects of long-term confinement in an institution, producing apathy, dependence, and boredom." Concerning this definition, Marty notes:

> Apathy greets churchly moralistic and dogmatic pronouncements on the left. Churchly dependence characterizes the sheep-like followers on the right. They actually welcome authoritarian shepherds who will prescribe their decisions for them. Meanwhile, boredom assaults the majority in the middle.

The primary definition of "institutionalize," however, is to "make into an institution." He cites James Gustafson's (a Protestant moral theologian) working definition: "An institution is a relatively persistent pattern of action or relationship in human society." In other words, an institution is a place where relationships are forged. At its best, people are formed, stretched and enriched by institutions, that is, by relating openly with caring people on a regular basis. Of another institution, marriage, W. H. Auden once wrote that "any marriage, however prosaic, is more interesting than any romance, however passionate." Marty argues that we need to keep closely linked the enthusiasm of the Spirit and the daily demands of forming community.

We need to challenge our young people to get over their boredom by personal involvement, by risking to witness their faith not only to their peers, but also to those with whom they work. We need to communicate more effectively to them that their deepest hunger is for God, and a real experience of love that is forever and forgiving. We need to show them what a difference the Church has made in our own lives. Friedrich Nietzsche, the nineteenth century atheist, once remarked of Christians, "they don't look very redeemed." A liturgist once said we appear too often as God's frozen people rather than God's chosen people. I am not calling only for enthusiasm; even more, I am calling for community grounded in faith. Adolescents long for community, friendship, identity and a challenge, a task that will take them out of themselves in the service of others. Even those drowning in materialism, realize that there has to be more. Surely, this can be found in the Church as a faith community.

It will help immensely if we can be candid with our students about our own shortcomings and those of the Church. We need to admit our institutional mistakes, e.g. Crusades, Inquisition, needless squelching of debate among professional theologians, and so on. Jesus guaranteed his Church freedom from error in essential teachings—he did not guarantee that it would be free from mistakes, stupidity or gross scandal on our part or on the part of our leaders—we have only to look at the Renaissance papacy to document dramatic lapses. A loving but refreshing candor will make it clear that we have nothing to hide—we are a pilgrim people made up of saints and sinners on our way to the Kingdom. If we approach our problems in this way students will, I believe, have less of a problem with the "institutional Church," and be more able to see its overwhelming positive side.

We need to be equally clear with our students about the truth of the divine guidance Christ has promised us. He promised us that "the gates of hell will not prevail against the Church" (Mt 16: 18). Whatever the inner conflicts of the Church, there will be, ultimately, a positive outcome. Belief in the Spirit's sure guidance will enable persons in the Church to move only slowly to final judgement about the ideas of other persons. Such a confident view of the Church will lead us to keep trying to communicate in loving, honest and open dialogue with our young people and with one another. The Gospel conversion and humility which Jesus taught are the ultimate secrets to harmonious living within the Church. As St. Augustine noted: "When we stop confessing our own sins we specialize in confessing the sins of others."

With these perspectives I hope it will be possible for teachers to help students see that the Church is the living presence of Jesus Christ in the world and as such is, as the Second Vatican Council taught, "the light of the world." Our teaching goals should be to foster faith in the mystery of the Church, to develop pride in its service to the Gospel and to invite active participation in the Church's life of worship, witness and service. After all, the very nature of the Church, for Catholics, is one in which visible signs—from the sacraments to faithful people to the Church and to Christ himself—all are present to form and strengthen each of us so that we might grow in age and grace and wisdom.

BUILDING A RELIGION CURRICULUM

Tom Zanzig

Helping to foster a sense of Catholic identity in the adolescents whom we serve is a major challenge for every religion teacher. It is not accomplished simply by developing/creating a list of Catholic concepts or dogmas and making certain that we put them into our curriculum.

In fact, the fostering of religious and faith growth is a task that belongs to the entire school rather than to the religion department alone. The particular role of formal religious instruction in the classroom can only be properly understood in light of a broader view of the faith transmission process. In this article I first briefly describe that larger process before commenting on the specific function within that process of the religion curriculum in the school.

One model for understanding how faith is passed on from one group or generation to another suggests that there are five related elements in that process that appear to function in a sequential fashion.

Fostering Catholic identity is part of the wider faith-transmission process. It is essential for us to see it in that context. For that purpose the following diagram may be helpful for it graphically illustrates the normal stages of faith formation:

```
                              R
                              E
                              C
Relational                    O
Ministry >>> Evangelization >>> G >>> Catechesis >>> Service
                              N
                              I
                              T
Pre-            Good News     I   Instruction and  Ministry to Others
Evangelization  Proclaimed    O   Explication      Sharing the Faith
                              N
```

1.   Relational Ministry: The whole process of faith transmission begins with the development of relationships of trust with young people. They must feel that they can trust us and that we are sympathetic to them and their concerns at this moment of their life. This is both a pre-evangelization activity and one that continues throughout the process.

Thomas Zanzig is a writer on adolescent catechesis for St. Mary's Press, Winona, MN. Adapted from a presentation.

2. *Evangelization*: This is the proclamation of the Good News of the unconditional and saving love of Jesus Christ. This is not a theological exercise but more a witness of what he has done and what his coming means in redeeming human history and individual lives. Evangelization is primarily a heart-to-heart rather than a head-to-head activity.

3. *Moment of Recognition*: At this point a response is required on the part of the student that indicates that they see in some way, however modest or inchoate, the personal relevance to them of Jesus' person and message. This is the beginning of "conversion," which is the desired response to evangelization.

4. *Catechesis*: This is a more systematic presentation of the riches of the Christian mystery and its application to life. Catechesis is an instruction shared with one who is now a believer—even though this faith may be very rudimentary. This catechesis often focuses on the sacramental initiation or celebration of the Christian mystery. It is not a notional or theoretical presentation but one aimed at making the initial faith "living, conscious and active" in the words of the Second Vatican Council (Decree on Bishops, #14). Later we shall treat of the relationship of this activity to "religious education."

5. *Service*: The Christian life spontaneously leads to action—faith in practice. This part of the process enables the believer to reflect in a practical way the mandate of Gospel love.

As noted, I believe that formal religious instruction, as well as religion curriculum planning, can only be properly understood within the context of this complex, wholistic process of faith formation. Our contemporary understanding of total youth ministry is a response to this reality. Having acknowledged this, we can begin to explore the particular and more narrow challenge of designing a religion curriculum that reflects and respects this process. As we begin this discussion, some introductory reflections are needed.

The first step in considering a religion curriculum in a Catholic school is to realize that there are implicit and explicit curricula, formal and informal curricula. For example, a school may teach more about justice and morality through its discipline program than is taught in a formal class on morality.

There is also the "silent" curriculum—the reality that we teach a lot of things by virtue of the things we decide not to teach. The things we exclude from our curriculum may be as significant as the things we include.

There is also the curriculum of the entire school where the notion of permeation of all subjects by Christian values needs to be offered as a key factor for the Catholic identity of the school.

If it were possible to come up with the ideal religion curriculum there would only be one available and we could simplify the whole process. The fact is there are many, many ways to develop a very fine religion curriculum. In this article, I will offer some focusing ideas and raise some issues. Those issues and focusing questions arise out of my own experience and my own reflection on it. They reflect as well *The Challenge of Adolescent Catechesis.*[1]

CLARITY ON GOALS

Let me first present a hierarchy of terms or set of distinctions that may be quite helpful in setting goals and objectives for a curriculum in religious education.

1. **Education in religion**
2. **Religious Education**
3. **Christian religious education**
4. **Catechesis**

1. **Education in Religion.** What I mean when I use this term is that it is possible to talk about religion with no attempt to proselytize, evangelize or convert anybody. Education in religion refers to the kind of education in religion that should be possible and happening in every public school in the country. Our young people have a right to an understanding of the religious history of humanity—as they have the right to its history, sociology, philosophy.

2. **Religious Education.** When we take "religion" and make it an adjective to describe the *kind* of educating we are doing, everything changes. In religious education, as I understand it, the believing community—an adult community committed to a certain religious tradition—consciously attempts to pass on their beliefs and practices. Because it is religious education it could be Jewish religious education, Buddhist religious education, etc.

3. **Christian Religious Education**. Here the presumption is that the adult community is one committed to the values of Jesus Christ. It is a community that is very consciously trying to evangelize and convert the next generation, to pass on their traditions. In Christian religious education, however, there is *not* the presumption that those people we are passing it on to are already evangelized and converted. In Christian religious education the presumption is that teachers are evangelized, converted and committed but they do not operate out of the presumption that their students are.

4. **Catechesis.** In catechesis, the presumption is that everybody involved in the enterprise—both the catechizers and the "catechizees"—are evangelized, converted and committed believers. When such characteristics are present everything—the curriculum content, method, relative roles of teacher and student—everything changes.

My personal bias is that the Catholic school religion teacher is primarily called to do Christian religious education. As believers they are teaching and witnessing to a Catholic faith in which they

24

personally deeply believe. They are not, however, assuming corresponding belief or commitment in the students.

Therefore the *primary* task of the classroom religion teacher is not to bring young people to a personal encounter with and commitment to Jesus. That may happen, of course, and it if does the teacher will give thanks to God because it is a great blessing for the student.

The teacher's role, however, in this context is to articulate what the community believes and practices so that students can understand what it is that they are being asked to make a decision about. The teacher's task is to communicate the knowledge, attitudes and skills that the Church expects in a believing and practicing Catholic. If the teacher does this well, he or she will contribute more to the student's personal faith development than they imagine.

In considering any particular religion theme or content an important question is: Given the students we are teaching, where in the hierarchy of approaches to teaching listed above, would we locate our effort? as a Christian religious educator? as a catechist?

If the topic were, for example, Jesus, one would treat this topic quite differently depending on whether the context is religious education or catechesis. As a religious educator you might foster an honest discussion about whether Jesus was the Son of God. That, however, is not a catechetical approach. In a catechetical approach— in which, again, the students are believers and committed—the approach might be to have the class study and pray John's Gospel to deepen their insights into the person and mystery of Jesus.

CURRICULUM BUILDING

Presuming clarity on these preliminary points, the work of curriculum building can begin. This task needs to reflect the following characteristics:
- theological integrity,
- sensitivity to the developmental patterns of adolescents, and
- recognition of both the opportunities and the limitations experienced in the parish and the school settings.

This article is not an attempt to simply share the results of my own thinking about the development of religion curriculums. Rather, I want to stimulate *your* reflection and/or discussion with members of the religion faculty at your school about this important dimension of the total ministry of the Catholic high school. The article presents a series of six questions for reflection and discussion, each suggesting a principle of design, intended to help us focus on our current religion curriculums.[2]

QUESTIONS FOR REFLECTION
AND DISCUSSION

1. **Does our religion curriculum provide a clear sequential and integrated presentation of the essential content of the Christian story and vision?**

This question is clearly loaded and deserves some elaboration. Implicit in the question are a number of my own personal convictions about curriculum development. In and of themselves, these convictions warrant some discussion, if not debate:

a.   There is a body of information about our Catholic Christian faith that is not arbitrary, and this information should be included in any curriculum that strives for theological integrity.

b.   The curriculum's content should unfold in a logical way, that is, with concepts in one course building in a sequential way upon concepts previously learned by the students.

c.   The entire curriculum should have some unifying principle, a clearly identified and recognizable "integrating thread" that weaves and connects the curriculum's courses into a reasonable whole.

As suggested, all of the above convictions are open to some debate. What they refer to and critique is a far too common situation: A school's religion curriculum has been allowed to simply evolve in a haphazard and, at times, even contradictory way over the years. The resulting "curriculum" is a series of courses with no apparent relationship to one another. Such a result will come about, for example, if courses are randomly incorporated into the curriculum purely on the basis of the experience or the biases of individual teachers. The answer to a question of why a particular course is part of the curriculum in such a school is that "at one time we had a teacher who was 'into' that topic." But the integrity of the curriculum can also be violated through omission rather than commission. That is, at times a central dimension of the Christian message might be avoided or eliminated because "we have no teacher able or willing to teach it." Neither including nor omitting courses purely on the basis of the experience or interests of teachers is acceptable if one of the characteristics we seek in our religion curriculums is theological integrity.

A related point should be raised here. There is no one, universal "integrating thread" that should always be present in every religion curriculum. If such unanimity across schools and religion faculties were possible or even desirable, there would be only one acceptable design for a religion curriculum. Such is clearly not the case. By way of example: For quite some time the integrating principle in many religion curriculums was the theme of *salvation history*. Commitment to this approach led many schools to offer a course on the Hebrew Scriptures to freshmen; the rationale for this was that all of salvation history could only be understood in light of the religious history of the Jews. However, more recently, an integrating principle in religion curriculums has been our emerging understanding of the *religious and faith development of adolescents*. Advocates of this approach base their curriculum designs on the evolving capacity of young people to understand and personally appropriate the content and meaning of Christian faith. Both approaches, as well as others, can be supported. The point is that a school should be able to identify what it is that integrates its religion courses into a reasonable curriculum. Can your religion faculty do that?

2. **Does your curriculum consider and reflect what we know about the religious and faith development of adolescents?**

I will readily admit that this question demonstrates my own bias towards sensitivity to student needs and abilities as a major integrating principle for developing a curriculum. My understanding of learning theory leads me to the strong conviction that failure to take into account the developmental characteristics of the potential learners virtually guarantees failure in the attempt to teach anything, religion included. This is not to suggest, in the context of our comments above, that material such as the Hebrew Scriptures cannot be taught to freshmen (though I do have my reservations on that point). The thrust of this principle is, however, that whatever we choose to teach at whatever grade level, the needs and abilities of the students should dictate at least how we teach the material. If a teacher is seeking a text for teaching the Hebrew Scriptures, he or she should not look for a text that simply covers the material adequately. The text must also be attuned to the starting point of the students with whom it will be used. Think about each one of your existing courses at each grade level: do the content and the processes incorporated into each course reflect a real sensitivity to the starting point of the students at that level of their development?

3. **In our curriculum, does the learning of concepts take precedence over the learning of facts?**

It is unfortunate that religion, like history, can be taught by having students simply memorize information, with little concern for whether or not they truly recognize and understand the significance and meaning of the concepts often hidden behind the information. This fact-oriented approach is far less likely to happen in the teaching of mathematics or the sciences; in those cases, the student's failure to understand one concept quickly shows up in the failure to understand a subsequent and dependent concept.

In the teaching of religion, though, we have to guard against the ease with which students can move from one course to another with little comprehension of the material presented. Methods for both the presentation of material and the testing of student understanding should be sensitive to this reality. For example, a lecture method of presentation followed by testing to determine if the students simply listened well—that is, whether they can give back the information as it was presented—tends to provide facts to the students while promoting little real learning. Group processes, personal reflection, open discussion, and approaches to testing that require more reflection than memorization (e.g., essay questions or the keeping of a journal) will lead to more effective learning of the theological content. Do the methods incorporated into your various religion courses foster learning rather than memorizing?

4. Are our students allowed and encouraged to question and honestly discuss what is being taught without fear of reprisal?

This question clearly deserves more discussion than I can give it here, so much so that I was tempted to avoid including it in this article. But I believe the question is simply too important to neglect. We have come to realize that the struggle to achieve maturity of faith nearly always demands that individuals experience what John Westerhoff calls "searching faith." The essential task of that search is for individuals to reevaluate their inherited religious beliefs, traditions, and practices in light of their increasing maturity. At some point, then, they freely choose whether or not to personally appropriate those culturally imposed religious realities into their own identities. At times this process can be very difficult, leading some individuals to a "crisis of faith"; for others the process can be relatively pain-free. In either case, the process appears to be essential to our growth as Christians. Does your religion curriculum help or hinder students in their journeys through "searching faith"?

5. Does our curriculum unfold in such a way that the students are prepared to assume personal responsibility for their continuing faith development beyond high school? Do we give them the skills they need in order to continue on with their faith development?

This question raises a number of related issues, among them the ultimate goals that we seek with our religion curriculum, our methodologies, and the skills we attempt to provide our students. Further questions may help us to more clearly focus on our ultimate goals: What kind of world will our students confront as they leave high school, and does their experience in our school provide them with the tools they will need to deal with that world as maturing Christians? These are tough questions, to be sure, but ones that get right to the heart of our efforts as religious educators of adolescents. Consider some others: Does our curriculum develop within the students a clear sense of their Catholic identity? Are our students learning how to pray? Can they find their way around the Scriptures, and can they interpret those Scriptures (to a reasonable extent), using acceptable approaches to biblical interpretation? Can our students make moral decisions that are grounded not in legalism but in a sound understanding of the values of Jesus? If we can answer such questions in the affirmative, we are on the right track. If not, perhaps we must reevaluate our entire curriculum, as well as the total life of the school—which brings us to our last question.

6. Is our religion curriculum understood within the context of the total life of the school community so that it both speaks to and is enhanced by the other dimensions of school life?

Again, as with question 5, the limitations of space preclude a lengthy discussion of this very important factor in our discussion of religious education in the Catholic high school. Suffice it to say that the attainment of the results implicit in question 5 above would seem to demand a commitment to a philosophy of campus ministry in the high school. Skills cannot simply be taught in classes; we learn what it means to live as Christians by doing it, not simply talking about it. Opportunities to engage in prayer, liturgical celebrations, retreats, service on behalf of peace and justice, peer ministry, and so on, are all vital to the adolescents' growth as Christians. On its own, a religion curriculum cannot lead students to Christian maturity, regardless of how well planned and implemented the curriculum is. Its primary task is to shed intellectual light on the realities of our faith. But these realities must be experienced in other areas of our lives—in relationships with family and peers, within our own personal experiences of the presence of God in our lives, within the context of communal worship, and more.

FOOTNOTES

1. The Challenge of Adolescent Catechesis, a project of the National Federation of Catholic Youth Ministry in collaboration with NCEA, NCDD and USCC, Washington, D.C., 1986.

2. The author has also developed a process for curriculum building that is available by writing him at Saint Mary's Press.

FACILITATING THE STUDENTS' SELF IMAGE

By Mark Link, S.J.

A distinguishing mark of a Catholic school is the presence of a faith atmosphere in which students and teachers alike discover and nurture the image of God in one another.

When I think of self image, I think of the story of a lion. Each day he would stand the crossroads of the jungle. As the animals filed by he would ask each one the same question: "Who's the king of the jungle?" And each day the animals would all give the same answer, "The lion is!" The lion would smile and the animals would continue on their way.

One day, an elephant came by. The lion bellowed out his usual question, "Who's the king of the jungle?" Now the elephant had heard about the lion's daily routine. And frankly, he didn't like it. So he decided he would not answer the lion's question. He would dramatize it.

He took his trunk, wrapped it around the lion's body, whirled the lion in the air, and threw him against the trunk of a huge oak tree. The lion hit the trunk with a "thud" and came crashing down to the ground in a heap. After a minute, the bewildered lion raised his head, blinked his eyes, and said to the elephant: "Well, you didn't have to get mad about it, just because you didn't know the answer."

Now that lion had a positive self image! I wish that the many young people I have taught in the past 25 years had that kind of self image. I also wish the teachers had that kind of self image.

WHY IS SELF IMAGE SO IMPORTANT?

As Catholic educators, we should be tremendously concerned about the self image. It is one of the marks that should distinguish our approach to education. Why? Consider just two reasons.

First, self image is the key to success in the *secular* world, which measures success in terms of one's ability to succeed. One of the most dramatic documentations of that was a study by Dr. Stanley Coopersmith, done years ago at the University of California. It involved nearly 2,000 young people, who were studied for six years from their early teens to their late teens. Coopersmith discovered that the single most important factor in determining how well young people performed in later life was the self image they developed in their formative teen years.

Rev. Mark Link, S.J., lecturer and author, writes religious educational materials for Tabor Press, Allen, TX. He resides at Canisius House, Evanston, IL.

This brings us to a second reason why self image is so important. It is also the key to success in the *christian* world, which measures success in terms of one's ability to love. It is a truism that if we don't love ourselves we cannot love another. The reason is clear: love is a self gift. If we do not see ourselves as loveable or valuable, we are not going to put a red ribbon around ourselves and give ourselves to someone we love. You don't give garbage to someone you like.

If Jesus' message of love is to take root in our world, we must help our young people—yes, even our teachers—to develop a positive self image.

How tragic for Catholic students—and Catholic teachers—to have a negative self image. Of all people, we are the ones who should have a positive self image. After all we believe that we are made in the image and likeness of God.

And so one of the distinguishing marks of a Catholic school is the presence of a faith atmosphere in which students and teachers alike discover and nurture the image of God in one another.

HOW IS SELF IMAGE SHAPED?

Frightening as it may seem, the people around us hold the key to our self image. This is so true that one psychologist, Bunaro Overstreet, did not hesitate to say, "We are not only our 'brother's keeper', we are also his maker." What he is saying is this. Our attitude toward other people, especially young people, influences greatly what they will become.

A German poet and dramatist, Johann von Goethe, put it this way: "Treat other people as if they were what they ought to be and you will help them to become what they are capable of being." A New York University sociologist, Robert Bierstadt, used to put the idea in an even more striking way: "I'm not who I think I am, and I'm not who you think I am, but I am who I think you think I am."

That is sometimes referred to as the "looking-glass" concept of self. It simply means that we derive our self image from other people. They act as a mirror reflecting back to us a self image that we eventually adopt as our own. For example, we walk into a room. As we do, everyone in the room lights up. They are saying to us, "We like you!" And we interpret this as meaning that there is something about us that is likeable and valuable.

On the other hand, we walk into a room. As we do, everyone glances up at us and continues doing what they were doing when we entered the room. They are saying to us, "We are indifferent toward you!" And we interpret this as meaning that there is nothing particularly likeable or loveable about us.

This brings us to the all-important question: "Concretely, what are some of the things that we can do, as Catholic teachers and educators, to help our students and each other develop a more

31

positive self image? More specifically, how can we go about building a faith atmosphere that will enable students and teachers to discover and nurture the image of God in which each is made?"

I would like to suggest five things. For the sake of emphasis, I will put them in question form.

Do we like our students?

Let me begin my remarks on love by saying this: "No one needs love more than someone who doesn't deserve it." If we wait around for students to become loveable before we love them, we will wait around for the rest of our lives. It is precisely in the process of being loved that students discover they are loveable. And only when they discover they are loveable, will they be able to give themselves in love.

And here let me say that it is often the externally "cool" students who need love the most. It is often the ones who give us the impression that they don't need our love, who are the ones who need it most.

At the start of my teaching career, someone gave me a poem by an anonymous author. It helped me tremendously on this point. The poem is called *Mask* and should be required reading for every Catholic school teacher and administrator. It reads:

Don't be fooled by me...
I wear a thousand masks—
masks that I am afraid to take off...
"For God's sake, don't be fooled.
I give the impression that I am secure...
that confidence is my name
and coolness my game...
and that I need no one.
Please don't believe me, please.
My surface may seem smooth,
but my surface is my mask...
"Beneath dwells the real me
in confusion, in fear, in aloneness...
That's why I frantically create a mask
to hide behind...to shield me
from the glance that knows.
But such a glance is precisely my salvation,
my only salvation...
That is, if it's followed by acceptance,
if it's followed by love...
"But I don't tell you this...
I'm afraid your glance will not be followed
by acceptance and love.
I'm afraid you'll think less of me,
that you'll laugh...

"So I play my game...
"I dislike the superficial game I'm playing...
I'd like to be really genuine...
But you've got to help me...
Each time
you're kind and gentle and encouraging,
each time you try to understand
because you really care,
my heart grows wings...
"I want you to know that.
I want you to know
how important you are to me.
How you can be the creator
of the person that is me, if you choose.
Please choose...
It will not be easy for you...
The nearer you approach
the blinder I might strike back...
I fight against the very thing I cry out for.
"But I am told that love is stronger
than the strongest walls,
and in this lies my hope.
MY ONLY HOPE..."

That poem contains a wealth of wisdom. If we could just live it out in our Catholic schools, we would incarnate in them the kind of love that Jesus himself showed toward people in his lifetime of teaching.

The point is this: Our students need our love. And they need it in a concrete, tangible way. In his book *If I Were Starting My Family Again*, John Drescher has a delightful story about a little six-year-old who finally got his own bedroom. Wouldn't you know it, the first night in his own room, there was a severe thunderstorm. He woke up and started shouting, "Daddy! Daddy! Come quickly. I'm afraid! I'm afraid!" His daddy shouted back, "Don't worry, son! God loves you! He'll take care of you." The boy shouted back, "I know God loves me. But right now I need somebody with skin on."

Little Bobby was right. There are times when we need somebody with skin on. And we need that skin pressed firmly against ours.

Teenagers, especially, need to now that they are loved by somebody with skin on. In his book, *Will the Real Me Please Stand Up?* John Powell recalls a time when a father confided to him that his son had been killed in a highway street accident. He composed a note on the night before his son was buried and placed it under the boy's body. It read:

My Dear Son:
I never told you how much I loved you. I never told you what a large part of my heart you occupied. I never told you what an important role in my life you played. I thought there would be a right time for this: when you graduated from school, when you would leave our home and set out on your own, when you got married. But now you are dead and there will ever be a right time. So I am writing this note and hoping that God will tell one of his angels to read this to you. I want you to know of my love for you, and my sorrow that I never told you of that love.
Your Dad.

The point is painfully clear. We need to express love toward one another in a concrete, tangible way. And this is especially true when it comes to young people—especially problem young people.

The model for the love we should have toward our students is Jesus himself. Paul puts it this way in Romans 5: 8-10 (TEV): "God has shown us how much he loves us—it was while we were still sinners that Christ died for us! ... We were God's enemies, but he has made us his friends through the death of his son." The way we can help our students develop a more positive self image: by doing for them what Jesus did for us.

This brings us to the second way we can help out students develop a more positive self image. Again, I put it in the form of a question.

Do we affirm our students?

Affirmation means that we encourage our students. We assure them that we think they have good qualities. We tell them that they have good qualities. We tell them verbally and non-verbally that we think they are special.

A few years ago, the film *Chariots of Fire* won the Academy Award for best film of the year. It concerned Eric Liddell, England's top 100-meter runner and a cinch to win the gold medal in the 1924 Paris Olympics. Deeply religious Eric never ran on a Sunday.

When the Olympic schedule was released, Eric was shocked. The 100-meter event was scheduled for Sunday. In spite of incredible pressure put on him by the British press, Eric refused to compete. He switched to the 400-meter race, a race he had never run in his life. To make a long story short, Eric won the gold medal in that event.

A prominent American runner in the same 1924 Olympics was Charlie Paddock. He also made a name for himself in Paris. When he returned home to Cleveland after the Olympics he was invited to speak to the students at East Tech High School. After the talk an excited student rushed up to him and said, "Gee, Mr. Paddock, I'd give anything to be an Olympic champion like you some day." Charlie looked at him and said, "Son, you can be anything you want, if you try hard enough." Twelve years later, that same student, Jesse Owens, won four gold medals for the U.S. team in the Berlin Olympics.

Jesse returned to the United States and was the guest of honor at a victory parade in Cleveland. When his car stopped, it was swamped by autograph seekers. One of them, a skinny young man, reached out excitedly and said, "Gee, Mr. Owens, I'd give anything to be an Olympic champion like you some day." Jesse squeezed the boys hand and said, "Son, you can be anything you want, if you try hard enough." Twelve years later, in 1948, the same young man, Harrison Dillard, tied Jesse's own record in the Olympic 100-meter dash in London.

Now that's affirmation with a vengeance! Few stories better illustrate its power. Here, again, the ones who need affirmation most are the scruffy ones—the ones who don't have a very positive self image.

Joseph Lahey was an eleven-year-old. He had a crippled back. It didn't look so bad when he was dressed. But when his shirt was off, it looked ugly. Joseph hated his back.

Now he stood in line with other boys in his class, waiting to be examined by the school doctor. He dreaded the moment when he would step into the examination room and the doctor would say, "Take off your robe." Finally, the terrible moment came. A stern, grey-haired man, sat behind a desk. He had a chart in his hand. After a few questions, the doctor said: "Now take off your robe!" Joseph fumbled with he cord. His hands were shaking badly. At last the robe was off.

The doctor looked at him and then did something unusual. He put down the chart, walked around the desk, cupped the boy's face in his big hands and looked straight into the boy's eyes. "Son," he said gently, "do you believe in God?" "Yes, sir," Joe replied. "Good!" said the doctor, "The more you believe in God, the more you believe in yourself." "Yes, sir," said Joe.

Then, just as suddenly as the doctor had shown this side of his character, he reverted back to his business-like side. He went back to his desk, wrote something on the chart, and left the room for a minute. Joe looked at the chart on the desk. He wondered what the doctor had written. Bracing himself for the worse, he moved forward and peeked at the chart. Under the heading "Physical Characteristics," the doctor had written five words: "Has an unusually well-shaped head." Joseph could hardly believe his eyes. Then the doctor returned. There were still a few little things to do. Then the doctor said with an understanding smile: "Okay, Joseph, you can put your robe back on and go. Please send in the next boy."

Joe never forgot the lesson the doctor taught him that day: "If we believe in God and focus on the best in ourselves, nothing can defeat us."

This is our job as Catholic teachers and administrators. It is to help the students deepen their faith in God and themselves. And one of the ways we help them do this is by affirmation.

I remember the principal of my own high school. He once asked me, "Mark, do you know what a good teacher is?" I said, "Well,

Mr. Noll, I know the teachers I like, but I'm not exactly sure what makes them so good." Mr. Noll replied, "A good teacher is one who sees through Johnny and sees Johnny through." I always remembered that statement. It is exactly what affirmation is. It's seeing through someone and, then, seeing them through—in terms of their strengths and their weaknesses.

No matter how poor a student is, we can always find something in them to affirm. I remember a father whose son came home with three Ds and two Fs. How are you going to affirm a kid like that? The father found a way. He said, "Well, son, one thing is certain. You're an honest guy. With a report card like that, you surely don't cheat!"

When it comes to poor students, I am reminded of a story about Michelangelo. As he was sculpting his masterpiece, David, a little boy watched fascinated. Day after day, the boy came and watched spellbound. Finally, the day came when David emerged from the block of marble. The boy approached Michelangelo and said, "Mister, how do you know there was a man inside that block of marble?"

There are plenty of blocks of marble sitting unsculpted in our classrooms. The trick is to see the man and the woman just aching to emerge from them. This is what affirmation is all about. It's calling forth the man and the woman from the students we teach.

Jesus was the model of affirmation. He said to a group of people on a hillside—plain folks, like the students we teach: "You are like salt for all mankind... You are like light for the whole world" (Mt 5:13-14).

This brings us to the third thing we can do to help students develop a better self image.

Do we believe in our students?

"Self-fulfilling prophesy"—that's a phrase you run into a lot these days. It simply means that a significant person's expectation of another person tends to get realized. For example, when Roger Bannister was training to try to break the four-minute mile, he really questioned whether he could do it. But his coach believed he could. Result? Roger became the first human being to run a sub four-minute mile. The decisive factor in Roger's accomplishment was his coach's faith in him.

Consider another example. Two teachers were given classes of equal ability. One was told, "You are in for a fantastic year!" The other was told, "You'll find out soon enough what kind of year you're in for." What happened to those two classes?

The first class outperformed the second in a resounding way. The first teacher really had a "fantastic year." When the principal asked the first teacher what she had done to make the class perform so brilliantly, she replied: "Well, to be honest, I couldn't miss. When I saw the IQs of those kids, I knew I was in for a fantastic year. Not a single IQ was under 120." The principal looked stunned and said, "But those numbers weren't the kids' IQs, they were the kids' locker numbers."

The teacher believed in those students, and they didn't let her down. One of the most important things we can do for our students is to believe in them—to believe in their ability, their goodness, their dreams. Andrew Greeley made this point eloquently a number of years back. Writing in *America* (6/4/64) magazine, he said:

> As I reflect back on my years of working with people... I regretfully concluded that I tended to miss the point completely. What young people...need more than anything else is encouragement. My blood chills when I think of all the young people I might have encouraged, whom I might have assured of their dignity and worth, in whom I might have made an act of faith, but failed to...because I did not see that this above all else was what they were seeking.
>
> I surely pointed out the goals for them and paid lip service to their ability to reach them. But in many instances I failed to understand that the fact that they did not strive for the goals was no indication that they did not value them or did not want them, but simply showed that they did not have enough faith in their own goodness to achieve what the goals imply. I admit in all honesty that it will be a long time before I will be able to excuse myself from this failure.

I agree with those words 100 percent.

Once again, our model in believing in our students—in their ability and in their goodness—is Jesus. "Whoever believes in me," Jesus told his disciples, "will do what I do—yes, he will do even greater things. I chose you and appointed you to go out and to bear much fruit" (Jn 14:12, 15:16).

This brings us to the fourth question.

Do we pray for our students?

Someone once said, "There comes a time when we must stop talking to our students about God and start talking to God about our students." I agree. I wish we all talked to God about our students as faithfully as we prepare our classes. Praying for our students is that important.

First, praying is a way of keeping sensitive to situations. The first year I ever taught was as a Jesuit seminarian at a high school in Detroit. I'll never forget that year. There were times when I was so tired I could not see straight. The hour meditation each day became a battle for me, just to keep awake. Another seminarian who was teaching with me at the same school was having the same problem I was. He told me later that he used to take his grade book and go down to the school gym to pray.

He would pace the gym floor, grade book in hand. He would read a name from the class list and then talk to God about that student. My friend was known for his high degree of sensitivity and skill in dealing with the students. I can't help but think that his way of praying for his students was largely responsible for this.

Let me share with you another story that touches on prayer. A young teacher named Mary wanted so much to succeed. But a student named Bill was turning her into a nervous wreck and her class into a three-ring circus. One morning before school, Mary was seated at her classroom desk writing something in shorthand. Suddenly Bill appeared at the door. "What are you writing?" he asked as he approached her desk. "I'm writing a prayer to God," she said. "Can God read shorthand?" he joked as he looked over her shoulder. "He can do anything," Mary said, "even answer this prayer." With that she tucked the prayer insider her bible and turned to write on the chalkboard. As she did, Bill transferred the prayer from her bible to his typing book.

Twenty years later Bill was going through a box of his belongings that his mother had stored in her attic. He came across his old typing book. Picking it up, he began to thumb through it. Lo and behold, he found the shorthand prayer. The paper on which it was written yellow and faded. Bill stared at the mysterious jottings and wondered what they said. He took the paper and put it in his wallet. When he got to his office, he gave the prayer to his secretary to decipher. She read it and blushed. "It's rather personal," she said. "I'll type it out and put it on your desk when I leave tonight." That night Bill read the prayer. It said:

Dear God, please don't let me fail this job. I can't handle my class with Bill upsetting it. Touch his heart. He's a boy who can become very good or very evil.

The final sentence hit Bill like a hammer. Only hours before, he was contemplating a decision that would compromise his integrity in a decisive way. He put the note in his wallet. During the next week, he reread it several times.

To make a long story short, that prayer caused Bill not to compromise his integrity. It did more. It prompted him to seek out his old teacher to tell her how her twenty-year-old prayer was finally answered in a most remarkable way.

Once again, Jesus is the model when it comes to prayer for our students. He prayed for his own disciples, saying, "I pray for them... I do not ask that you take them out of the world, but I do ask you to keep them safe from the Evil One" (Jn 17:9,15).

This brings us to the final point.

Do we deal with our students creatively?

It is so easy to call upon authority in taxing situations. It is so much more effective to call upon ingenuity. Consider an example.

A high school teacher in New Jersey told his class about a rigged TV show that scandalized the nation years ago. To his surprise most of the students didn't think a rigged TV show was anything to get upset about. So what if it was rigged? It's a TV show. The TV people can do anything they want. After all, it is their show.

It was obvious to the teacher that there was no point in prolonging the discussion. The students had made up their minds and that was it.

About a week later, the teacher gave the class a test. He rigged it and gave a handful of students (poor students, at that) advance help on the test. When the other students learned what had happened, they were furious: "You're not serious about that test!" He replied, "Dead serious!" "You're going to count it?" the students asked. "Of course, I'm going to count it!" he replied. "But that's not fair," they chorused back. "Look," said the teacher, "I can do anything I want. It's my class!"

The students got the point. When lying, stealing, or cheating do not touch us, we can be very casual about them. But when they touch us, it's a different story.

That teacher got across an important lesson in a creative, effective way.

Jesus himself was a model of creativity. We see it time after time in the parables he taught. He used stories of fish, lost coins, runaway boys, and thieves to teach his students. These stories not only taught people, but challenged them in a non-threatening way. Jesus rarely pointed a finger at anyone. He simply told a creative story and let the people figure it out themselves. In short, Jesus respected people. And we should do the same with our students.

Let me conclude my remarks about creativity with a personal story. Years ago I was teaching undergraduates at Loyola University in Chicago. I always knew when the applications for acceptance into medical school had been sent back to the students. Four or five students were always devastated. It was clear that I had to deal with this. I tried many times to reason with the unsuccessful students: "Maybe this setback will turn out to be a blessing in disguise. You're still young. You still have time to get into a different field." But nothing I said seemed to get through. Then one day, I got the idea to use a story to try to make my point with them. Let me share it with you.

Eugene Orowitz didn't have much going for him. He was a skinny, 100 pound sophomore at Collingswood High in Collingswood, New Jersey. One afternoon the gym coach held classes in the middle of the track field. He wanted to show the kids how to throw the javelin. After the coach finished his instructions, he let the kids try their hand at throwing it. When it came time for Eugene to throw, the kids laughed. "Hey, Ugly, can you lift it?" someone shouted. "Careful! You'll stab yourself," another shouted.

A strange feeling came over Eugene as he stood there listening to the jeers. He had watched the coach closely and was a good mimic. He raised the javelin over his head, took six quick steps and let it fly. It soared 20, 30, 40, 50 yards. Then it crashed into the empty bleachers. It turned out to be the longest throw of the day. When Eugene retrieved the javelin, the coach noticed that the tip was broken. "Orowick, you broke the javelin! It's no good to us now. You broke it; you get rid of it."

Eugene took the javelin home. That summer Eugene threw the javelin hour after hour and day after day in a vacant lot next to his home. To make a long story short, he became skilled in throwing it. At the end of his senior year, he threw it 211 feet, farther than any high school student in the nation.

Eugene got a scholarship to the University of Southern California. He began dreaming of the Olympics. Then one day he didn't warm up properly and tore the ligaments in his shoulder. That put an end to javelin throwing, his scholarship, and his dreams. All his hard work went down the drain. It was as if God had slapped him in the face after he had performed a minor miracle with his 100-pound body. Eugene dropped out of college and took a job in a warehouse.

One day, Eugene met a struggling actor who asked him to help him with his lines. Eugene got interested in acting himself and enrolled in an acting school. Again, to make a long story short, he got his first big acting break when he was cast as Little Joe Cartwright in "Bonanza." That show ran 14 years on TV. Later, he got the lead in another long-run show, "Little House on the Prairie." Now he writes, directs, and acts in his own network show, "Highway to Heaven."

Today, Michael Landon, whose real name is Eugene Orowitz, will tell you that the best thing that ever happened to him was the day he tore his ligaments in his shoulder. What seemed to be an incredible tragedy turned out to be an incredible blessing. It guided him into a new life that surpassed his fondest dreams.

Landon's story got across the point I wanted to make. It did more! I did it in a *creative* way that *touched* the students deeply.

CONCLUSION

As Catholics we believe that we are made in the image and likeness of God. Our Catholic schools must reflect this fact. Concretely, this means that a primary concern of Catholic educators must be to create in our schools an atmosphere where teachers and students alike can discover and nurture the image of God in another. More specifically, it means creating an atmosphere of love, affirmation, faith, prayer and creativity. Only in such an environment will true Catholic education take place.

JUSTICE AND PEACE:
CONSTITUTIVE ELEMENTS
OF CATHOLICITY
Sr. Loretta Carey, R.D.C.

When one raises questions about the identity of the Catholic high school today, one raises theological and ecclesiological questions as well as situational ones. Changing definitions of mission, evangelization, education, church, and theological method are compounded by changing patterns of ownership, governance, staffing, finance and student population.

Concerning this creative chaos, one clear statement can be made. Justice and peace (as virtues, values, questions, answers; as cognitive, affective, and behavioral goals; as content, method, structure, policy, curriculum and extra curricula) have emerged as constitutive elements of Catholicity and therefore of education in the Catholic high school.

This phenomenon results from articulation by the Church over the past century, with increasing clarity, precision, power and insistence, that gospel values must be applied anew in a rapidly changing world.

Science has provided a technological capacity for both great progress and great disaster. Communication has made the world a "global village." But neither science nor communication can provide the ethics, morality, vision or spiritual energy for the journey toward a world of justice, peace, truth and love for which humanity longs. The Gospel of Jesus Christ can!

Catholic social teaching is essentially a reflection by the Church on the experience of peoples everywhere.[1] It examines and describes this human situation and applies gospel values and the wisdom of the social tradition to the "new moment."[2]

The Vatican II document *The Church in the Modern World* states that the Church is in the world as the "sign and safeguard of the dignity of the human person." That dignity, achieved in community, is the focus of social teaching in our day.

Beginning in 1891 with *Rerum Novarum* as a response to the new situation caused by the industrialization of the European agricultural economy, Catholic social teaching articulated the rights of workers to a just wage, to human working conditions and to organize to achieve these rights.

After World War II, *Pacem in Terris* developed the philosophy of rights flowing from human dignity, and emphasized, in the search for peace on earth, the need for structures of public authority to act world-wide to promote the universal common good. Paul VI called

Sr. Loretta Carey, R.D.C., has been director of the Fordham Center for Justice and Peace at Fordham University, New York, NY.

attention to the growing gap between affluent and poor nations. John Paul II has pointed out the dignity of labor and has connected the right to work with human dignity and with the building of the kingdom. Recently, in *On Social Concerns* he has given new analysis of superpower conflicts in the North, and to their political, military and economic effect on the less developed countries of the South. This, he has called a "structure of sin."

In addition, national bishops' conferences have applied Church teaching to more local situations; for example, the U.S. bishops letters on war and peace, the U.S. economy, and race.

This powerful Catholic perspective on social issues afforded by these documents needs to become a part of the intellect and heart of our students.

Recent documents on Catholic education have all stated that church social teaching should be a part of this effort. The latest from the Congregation for Catholic Education, *The Religious Dimensions of Education in a Catholic School* (1988) notes the integrating potential of social teaching.

> Christian social ethics must be founded on faith. From this starting point, it can shed light on related disciplines such as law, economics, and political science, all of which study the human situation, and this is an obvious area for fruitful interdisciplinary study...(#88) These then are the basic elements of a Christian social ethic; the human person, the central focus of the social order; justice, the recognition of the rights of each individual; honesty, the basic condition for all human relationships; freedom, the basic right of each individual and of society. World peace must then be founded on good order and the justice to which all men and women have a right as children of God; national and international well-being depend on the fact that the goods of the earth are gifts of God, and are not the privilege of some individuals or groups while others are deprived of them. Misery and hunger weigh on the conscience of humanity and cry out to God for justice. (#89) This then is an area which can open up broad possibilities. Students will be enriched by the principles and values they learn, and their service of society will be more effective. The Church supports and enlightens them with a social doctrine which is waiting to be put into practice by courageous and generous men and women of faith. (#90)

THE PROBLEM

To date, the Catholic school has not been in the forefront of Church institutions which have sought to respond to social teaching. Although there have been responses:

- some are symbolic; at the level of lip-service or at the interest of an individual teacher;
- some are strategic; more integral to the religion department at least, or more widely accepted by teachers who have had some significant in-service experience such as the infusion workshop for justice/peace education;
- none are instrumental as yet. Social teaching is not the vehicle

by which the educational mission of the school is accomplished. This would be the role of social teaching as a constitutive element of the Catholic school identity.

The 1985 research *Sharing the Faith: The Belief and Values of Catholic High School Teachers* noted that of 22 life goals presented to Catholic secondary teachers, only four related to concerns about social justice and world peace.[3] By all teachers these were ranked:

- combat racism   12
- promote economic and social justice   13
- promote world peace   14
- change economic policies which
  oppress people in other countries   18

The first three ranked in the middle range of teacher priority. The fourth, dealing specifically with social change, ranked quite low. The only goals which ranked lower were:
- to have more money than I have now
- to have an exciting, fulfilled life
- to be well-liked
- to do whatever I want to do when I want to do it.
In commenting on this finding, the author states:

Our research adds an additional and perhaps unexpected question. Why do all teachers, religion and lay, report limited enthusiasm for issues of social justice and peace? Do their responses indicate rejection or unfamiliarity with the Church's social teaching? Whether the report indicates a rejection of language or an indifference to the concept of action on behalf of justice, this report strongly suggests that the Catholic high school needs to consider ways to strengthen its faculty commitment to form "men and women who will make the civilization of love a reality."[4]

Obviously, faculty commitment must precede action to make justice and peace a constitutive element of the Catholic identity of the school.

My own experience of the past 12 years supports these research findings. Part of my work has been to try to define peace and justice education, to dialogue with teachers and administrators, and to act as a catalyst (often in in-service workshops for teachers) for the personal, organizational and curricular changes required by this goal. I have concluded:

1. Social documents of the Church are not yet perceived by teachers as important to themselves or their curriculum, or to their role as educators. Far from being worthy of reflective reading and discernment, they provide many Catholic teachers with grounds for debate.

2. There are serious pockets of active resistance in every faculty to the notion of Catholic social teaching; discomfort that the pope or bishops should or could say anything about these matters; lack of agreement that social teaching should be part of the identity of

the Catholic school and its program.

3. There are vast areas of non-response within faculties, which arise from a lack of information about social teaching, from indifference, hopelessness, overwork or lack of creative imagination in applying these teachings and values to instruction.

Typically, the departments in Catholic secondary schools are quite discreet for historical, philosophical or practical reasons. Also typically, "religion" becomes one of these departments. This division does not facilitate the development of an integrated curriculum with gospel values and social teaching as its core.

THE CHALLENGE FOR CATHOLIC SCHOOLS

Catholic educators can do more, do differently and do better than we have in making justice and peace integral and instrumental in our education.

1. We can focus on the qualities of the persons we hope to be graduating and the competencies they need to live a gospel life in our day.

2. We can gain some consensus on the fact that no education is value free and on a statement of the underlying values of Catholic social teaching.

3. We can commit to promoting the unity of knowledge through inter-disciplinary learning.

4. We can agree to develop in our students a sense of life goals and career objectives which include participation in economic, political and cultural life but which also include responsibility for transforming these structures when they oppose human dignity and community.

5. We can develop a conceptual framework from social teaching which each discipline can explicitate in ways appropriate to it.

6. We can include action for service and change as part of the curriculum.

7. We can turn our attention to the formation of students as well as to the information of course content.

Focusing the attention of teachers on student formation can, in my experience, overcome some resistance or indifference to "peace and justice" (as educational responses to the church's social teachings have come to be called). Content, method and value questions will arise, but within a context of shared agreement on student competencies.

A Catholic secondary school seeking to promote this element of Catholic identity could make an adequate response to the Church's social teaching by adopting these competencies as the central focus of an interdisciplinary effort:

1. **Social Imagination**

Being able to imagine a better and different world, a world of peace, justice and dignity is the first skill I propose. Imagination energizes for change and defeats the feelings of powerlessness, confusion and guilt which sometimes overwhelms young people as they look at the world. For example, the U.S. Bishops' Peace Pastoral opens with a section on the themes to develop social imagination. Imagination can build the political will on which change depends.

2. **Perspective Taking**

Students need to look at the world and its issues from other points of view besides their own. The ability to take a more global perspective is a function of "catholicity." A shift in perspective on issues is indeed necessary for U.S. Catholics to respond to John Paul II's suggestion in *On Social Concerns* that the East-West rivalry of the two superpowers is being played out in surrogate countries in the third world.

3. **Structural Analysis**

Many people, including people of faith, attribute evil in the world to personal causes only (e.g. if people are poor, it is because they are lazy). Catholic social teaching requires an understanding and analysis of structural realities also (e.g. poverty may stem from unemployment or racial prejudice). The church calls on its members for actions to change structures when these oppose human dignity. "Among the actions and attitudes opposed to the will of God and the good on consuming desire for profit; and on the other, the thirst for power with the intention of imposing one's will upon others...at any price. It is a question of a moral evil, the fruit of many sins, which lead to "structures of sin." To diagnose the evil in this way is to identify precisely, on the level of human conduct, the path to be followed in order to overcome it." (*On Social Concerns*, #37)

4. **Cultural Critique**

Catholic students must be helped to understand the profound relationship between faith and culture. They must be able to recognize the positive and negative elements of U.S. culture—to participate in the former and to resist the latter. "Hidden behind certain decisions, apparently inspired only by economics or politics, are real forms of idolatry; of money, ideology, class, technology...what is hindering full (human) development is that desire for profit and that thirst for power." The obstacles to integral development rest on more profound attitudes which human beings can make into absolute values. (SRS #38)

5. **Conflict Resolution**

In our time, technology capacity seems to have outrun ethical capacity. We have invented weapons which can indiscriminately destroy human life and its environment, but we have no ethic to deal with this new capacity. Alternatives to violence must be developed to process human conflicts. Teaching conflict resolution skills to students provides personal life skills, but also develops a political will which resists violence and insists on alternative measures to resolve human conflict on the local and international levels. The U.S. Bishops stated: "To teach the ways of peace is not to 'weaken the nation's will' but to be concerned for the nation's soul." (p. 324 *Origins* vol. 12, no. 20) The bishops supported the findings of a commission which concluded "peace is a legitimate field of learning that encompasses rigorous inter-disciplinary research, education and training towards peacemaking expertise." They strongly urged citizens to support training in conflict resolution. (p. 319)

6. Co-operative Skills

Competitive individualism is a characteristic of U.S. society. When it serves to divide and isolate, it needs to be counteracted, but sometimes unfortunately some characteristics of the Catholic secondary school can reinforce this problem. How can Catholic schools promote cooperation and solidarity which result in the enhancement of unity and community? Faculties should take time to examine the school's culture and minimize competition where possible.

Educational researchers at Johns Hopkins and at the University of Minnesota have developed systems for cooperative learning which could promote the attitudes and skills to address this cultural problem. The U.S. bishops stated: "America needs a new experiment in cooperation and collaboration. Such an experiment has a moral and cultural aspect; the renewal and enhancement of the sense of solidarity we have discussed above." *(Justice for All*, #242.)

7. Participation

Catholic schools should provide students both opportunity and skills for involvement in school, civic and global organizations. Knowing how to promote what is good and transform what is evil or inadequate is a practical response to the social vision of the gospel. Committee work, leadership skills, organizing, lobbying, advocacy or even resistance should be part of our students' repertoire of skills. In the economic pastoral, as one example of the call for participation, the bishops write: "The process of forming national economic policies should encourage and support contributions of all the different groups that will be affected by them." (#266)

The Catholic identity of the secondary school could indeed be enhanced by doing between what is already being done in religious formation; theology classes, retreat programs, liturgical participation, prayer opportunities, counseling and the process of caring adult models.

However, I believe that an adequate Catholic identity for our times will only result from a total faculty effort involving all disciplines. Language arts, communications, social studies, foreign languages, science, math, art and music can provide an integrated world view—a common vision of our world and of life's meaning if the concepts and skills of academic discipline are infused and integrated by Catholic social teaching.

FOOTNOTES

1. Henriot, Peter, Edward Deberri and Michael Schultheis. *Catholic Social Teaching: Our Best Kept Secret.* Orbis Books, Maryknoll NY, 1988.

2. *The Challenge of Peace: God's Promise and Our Response.* U.S. Catholic Conference, Washington, DC 1983.

3. Benson, Peter, Michael Guerra, *Sharing the Faith: The Beliefs and Values of Catholic High School Teachers.* NCEA, Washington, DC, 1985.

4. *Sacred Congregation for Catholic Education, Lay Catholics in the Schools*, Daughters of St. Paul, Boston, MA, 1983, p. 13.